Author's I

This book features 100 influential and inspiring quotes by Benjamin Franklin. Undoubtedly, this collection will give you a huge boost of inspiration.

1

"Either write something worth reading or do something worth writing."

2

"Three may keep a secret, if
two of them are dead."

3

"They who can give up essential liberty to obtain a little temporary safety deserve neither liberty nor safety."

4

"Tell me and I forget, teach me and I may remember, involve me and I learn."

5

"He that can have patience
can have what he will."

6

"You may delay, but time will not."

7

"A Penny Saved is a Penny Earned"

8

"In wine there is wisdom, in beer there is Freedom, in water there is bacteria."

"Many people die at twenty five and aren't buried until they are seventy five."

10

"Never ruin an apology with an excuse."

"We are all born ignorant, but one must work hard to remain stupid."

12

"Justice will not be served until those who are unaffected are as outraged as those who are."

13

"Fear not death for the sooner we die, the longer we shall be immortal."

"I didn't fail the test, I just found 100 ways to do it wrong."

15

"By failing to prepare, you are preparing to fail."

16

"Those who would give up essential liberty to purchase a little temporary safety, deserve neither liberty nor safety."

17

"Beer is proof that God loves
us and wants us to be happy."

18

"How many observe Christ's birthday! How few, His precepts!"

19

"Being ignorant is not so much a shame, as being unwilling to learn."

20

"Hide not your talents, they for use were made. What's a sundial in the shade?"

21

"Well done is better than well said."

22

"An investment in knowledge always pays the best interest."

"It is the first responsibility of every citizen to question authority."

24

"Lost Time is never found again."

25

"Instead of cursing the darkness, light a candle."

"If all printers were determined not to print anything till they were sure it would offend nobody, there would be very little printed."

"The Constitution only guarantees the American people the right to pursue happiness. You have to catch it yourself."

28

"Be at war with your vices, at peace with your neighbors, and let every new year find you a better man."

"Remember not only to say the right thing in the right place, but far more difficult still, to leave unsaid the wrong thing at the tempting moment."

"Tis a great confidence in a friend to tell him your faults; greater to tell him his."

"The person who deserves most pity is a lonesome one on a rainy day who doesn't know how to read."

"Dost thou love life? Then do not squander time, for that's the stuff life is made of."

"Early to bed and early to rise makes a man healthy, wealthy, and wise."

34

"Never confuse Motion with Action."

"Educate your children to self-control, to the habit of holding passion and prejudice and evil tendencies subject to an upright and reasoning will, and you have done much to abolish misery from their future and crimes from society."

"He that is good for making excuses is seldom good for anything else."

37

"Whatever is begun in anger,
ends in shame."

38

"Do not anticipate trouble, or worry about what may never happen.
Keep in the sunlight."

"The heart of a fool is in his mouth, but the mouth of a wise man is in his heart."

40

"There was never a bad peace
or a good war."

41

"Whoever would overthrow the liberty of a nation must begin by subduing the freeness of speech."

"Be slow in choosing a friend, slower in changing."

43

"Love your Enemies, for they tell you your Faults."

"We must all hang together, or assuredly we shall all hang separately."

45

"When you are finished changing, you're finished."

46

"To find out a girl's faults, praise her to her girlfriends."

"When you're testing to see how deep water is, never use two feet."

48

"If you fail to plan, you are planning to fail!"

"An ounce of prevention is worth a pound of cure."

50

"A slip of the foot you may soon recover, but a slip of the tongue you may never get over."

51

"Trouble knocked at the door, but, hearing laughter, hurried away"

52

"Life biggest tragedy is that we get old too soon and wise too late"

"When the people find that they can vote themselves money that will herald the end of the republic."

54

"If Jack's in love, he's no judge
of Jill's beauty."

"Happiness depends more on the inward disposition of mind than on outward circumstances."

"Keep your eyes wide open before marriage, half shut afterwards."

57

"If you would not be forgotten, as soon as you are dead and rotten, either write things worth reading, or do things worth writing."

58

"In the Affairs of this World
Men are saved, not by Faith,
but by the Lack of it."

"Who is wise? He that learns from everyone. Who is powerful? He that governs his passions. Who is rich? He that is content. Who is that? Nobody."

"Be civil to all; sociable to many; familiar with few; friend to one; enemy to none."

"My refusing to eat flesh occasioned an inconveniency, and I was frequently chided for my singularity, but, with this lighter repast, I made the greater progress, for greater clearness of head and quicker comprehension. Flesh eating is unprovoked murder."

"We do not stop playing because we grow old, we grow old because we stop playing!"

63

"If a man could have half of his wishes, he would double his troubles."

"Speak ill of no man, but speak all the good you know of everybody."

"Were I a Roman Catholic, perhaps I should on this occasion vow to build a chapel to some saint, but as I am not, if I were to vow at all, it should be to build a light-house.

66

"While we may not be able to control all that happens to us, we can control what happens inside us."

"Never leave till tomorrow
that which you can do today."

"The best thing to give to your enemy is forgiveness; to an opponent, tolerance; to a friend, your heart; to your child, a good example; to a father, deference; to your mother, conduct that will make her proud of you; to yourself, respect; to all others, charity."

"A house is not a home unless it contains food and fire for the mind as well as the body."

"Work as if you were to live a thousand years, play as if you were to die tomorrow."

71

"The way to see by faith is to shut the eye of reason."

72

"Security without liberty is called prison."

"Contentment makes poor
men rich,
Discontent makes rich men
poor."

"All mankind is divided into three classes: those that are immovable, those that are movable, and those that move."

"When the well is dry, we know the worth of water."

"The only thing that is more expensive than education is ignorance."

"It takes many good deeds to build a good reputation, and only one bad one to lose it."

"To be humble to superiors is a duty, to equals courtesy, to inferiors nobleness."

"Don't put off until tomorrow
what you can do today."

80

"A Brother may not be a Friend, but a Friend will always be a Brother."

"Eat to live, don't live to eat."

82

"Fish and visitors smell in
three days."

83

"...there will be sleeping
enough in the grave...."

84

"Beware of little expenses; a small leak will sink a great ship."

85

"Fools make feasts and wise men eat them."

86

"He who can have patience
can have what he will."

87

"Words may show a man's wit, actions his meaning."

88

"You will find the key to success under the alarm clock."

"There are three things extremely hard: steel, a diamond, and to know one's self."

"For the best return on your money, pour your purse into your head."

"Tricks and treachery are the practice of fools that don't have brains enough to be honest."

"So convenient a thing to be a reasonable creature, since it enables one to find or make a reason for every thing one has a mind to do."

"Reading makes a full man, meditation a profound man, discourse a clear man."

"How few there are who have courage enough to own their faults, or resolution enough to mend them."

"No one cares what you know until they know that you care!"

"A good example is the best sermon."

"You can do anything you set your mind to."

"Many a man thinks he is buying pleasure, when he is really selling himself to it."

99

"Happiness consists more in the small conveniences of pleasures that occur every day, than in great pieces of good fortune that happen but seldom to a man in the course of his life."

"Anger is never without a reason, but seldom with a good one."

Printed in Great Britain
by Amazon

16703703R00058